SHADOW OF THE OWL

Matthew Sweeney (1952-2018) was born in Lifford, Co. Donegal, Ireland. He moved to London in 1973 and studied at the Polytechnic of North London and the University of Freiburg. After living in Berlin and Timisoara for some years, he returned to Ireland and settled in Cork. He died in 2018 from motor neurone disease.

His poetry collections include: *A Dream of Maps* (Raven Arts Press, 1981); *A Round House* (1983) and *The Lame Waltzer* (1985) from Allison & Busby / Raven Arts Press; *Blue Shoes* (1989) and *Cacti* (1992) from Secker & Warburg; *The Bridal Suite* (1997), *A Smell of Fish* (2000), *Selected Poems* (2002), *Sanctuary* (2004) and *Black Moon* (2007) from Jonathan Cape; *The Night Post: A Selection* (Salt, 2010); *Horse Music* (2013), *Inquisition Lane* (2015), *My Life as a Painter* (2018) and *Shadow of the Owl* (2020) from Bloodaxe; and *King of a Rainy Country* (2018) from Arc, a book of prose poems set in Paris, and responding to Baudelaire's *Le Spleen de Paris*.

Horse Music won the inaugural Pigott Poetry Prize in association with Listowel Writers' Week, and was a Poetry Book Society Recommendation. *Black Moon* was shortlisted for the T.S. Eliot Prize and for the *Irish Times* Poetry Now Award. He also published editions of selected poems in Canada (*Picnic on Ice*, Vehicule Press, 2002) and two translated by Jan Wagner in Germany, *Rosa Milch*, (Berlin Verlag, 2008) and *Hund und Mond* (Hanser Berlin, 2017). Jan Wagner's German translation of *Shadow of the Owl* is forthcoming from Hanser Berlin.

He won a Cholmondeley Award in 1987 and an Arts Council Writers' Award in 1999. He also published poetry for children, with collections including *The Flying Spring Onion* (1992), *Fatso in the Red Suit* (1995) and *Up on the Roof: New and Selected Poems* (2001). His novels for children include *The Snow Vulture* (1992) and *Fox* (2002). He edited *The New Faber Book of Children's Poems* (2003) and *Walter De la Mare: Poems* (2006) for Faber; co-edited *Emergency Kit: Poems for Strange Times* (Faber, 1996) with Jo Shapcott; and co-wrote *Writing Poetry* (Teach Yourself series, Hodder, 1997) and the novel *Death Comes for the Poets* (Muswell Press, 2012) with John Hartley Williams.

MATTHEW SWEENEY

Shadow of the Owl

BLOODAXE BOOKS

ISBN: 978 1 78037 542 7

First published 2020 by
Bloodaxe Books Ltd,
Eastburn,
South Park,
Hexham,
Northumberland NE46 1BS.

www.bloodaxebooks.com
For further information about Bloodaxe titles
please visit our website and join our mailing list
or write to the above address for a catalogue

Supported using public funding by

**ARTS COUNCIL
ENGLAND**

Cover design: Neil Astley & Pamela Robertson-Pearce.

Printed in Great Britain by Bell & Bain Limited, Glasgow, Scotland, on
acid-free paper sourced from mills with FSC chain of custody certification.

CONTENTS

OTHER POEMS

ACKNOWLEDGEMENTS

Thanks are due to the editors of the following publications in which some of these poems appeared: *The Dark Horse, The High Window, The Irish Times, Magma, The Moth, The North, PN Review, Poetry, Poetry International, Poetry London, Southword* and *The Spectator*.

Thanks to Hans Van Eijk of Bonnefant Press (NL) for publishing the poem 'The Owl' in a hand-set limited edition in 2018 and for all his support of Matthew's work over the years.

Thanks to Neil Astley, the publisher who validated Matthew's life's work by offering his poetry a safe harbour in the last ten years of his life.

Thanks to the publishers John Lucas and Peter Sansom, and the editor Bill Swainson, for their unrelenting friendship and support.

Matthew was blessed in the friends he had gathered around him; these were, inevitably, friends in poetry, as well as in life. I know he would want to acknowledge all the people who were his steadfast allies over the years. Thank you.

And although it may seem invidious to single out the few from the many, I'd like to thank in particular Matthew's poetry friends in Cork, including Gerry Murphy, Pat Cotter, Thomas McCarthy, Dean Browne and Crónán Ó Doibhlin. Old friends Joe Mallon and Aidan Murphy kept the poetry conversations going in Dublin and Monaghan.

Jo Shapcott, Thomas Lynch, Christopher Reid, Pádraig Rooney, David O'Meara and Jan Wagner all worked closely with Matthew, and he greatly valued these creative friendships.

John Hartley Williams (1942-2014) was the first reader of much of Matthew's work, and the friend whom Matthew mourned until the end of his own life.

Maurice Riordan was the unstinting friend on whose deep loyalty and wisdom Matthew relied.

Heartfelt thanks to David O'Meara who assisted Matthew in the editing of some of the poems in this collection.

Think where man's glory most begins and ends,
And say my glory was I had such friends.

W.B. YEATS, 'The Municipal Gallery Revisited'

[MN]

FOREWORD

Matthew Sweeney was diagnosed with Motor Neuron Disease in October 2017; he died a mere ten months later, in August 2018. Most of the poems in this collection were written in that period, and it now seems as if his entire life in poetry – he published twelve full collections in his lifetime – was preparation for this final work.

A long poem, 'The Owl', is the wellspring from which the book emerged. The twelve stanzas of this poem were written over as many nights, in September 2017, as Matthew waited for the final diagnosis. In order to process his fear, he imagined a menacing owl coming, nightly, to the garden, but refusing to be seen and refusing to deliver his message. Matthew didn't know where the poem wanted to take him, but his habit of writing directly from his unconscious came to his aid as he sat, night after night, converting his distress into episodes in the history of the taciturn owl. The poem proved to be premonitory: when the diagnosis did come, on the afternoon of 11 October 2017, it was delivered, by an unseen neurologist, via mobile phone. Matthew was at the bookies when he got the call, and he stumbled out into the street, narrowly missing being crushed by a passing car.

> Did he think I could wait forever, as if I were
> a rock? I sliced some cheddar and a heel of bread,
> opened the back door and went out. The moon
> turned his big eye onto me, and I saw him wobble.
> The stars hummed along. *Where am I going?*
> I shouted at all of them. There was no response.
> Then far off, I heard a faint *huhuhu* followed by
> a *whoo*. *You cowardly bastard!*, I roared, and
> sprayed the arrows all over the blackened world.
>
> ('The Owl')

Although the cowardly neurologist failed to look his patient in the eye, the poet did not shy away from the task facing him. In the ten months that remained to him, he produced his last book, a sequence of dark fables charting the peregrinations of a hapless figure hounded by a procession of invisible enemies who want him dead. The poet was writing for his life.

The sphere of action is reduced to the gardens and banks of the River Lee in Cork, in the company of the cats and birds that inhabit the suburban garden – the wild, fugitive days spent navigating the murky borderlands of Central and Eastern Europe are but a memory. But the imaginative scope of the poems is undiminished – if anything, the persona on the run in these poems needs to reach new heights of ingenuity, to become even more inventive and wily, if he is to escape – just – the most horrible of deaths, over and over again.

All of Sweeney's verve and spiky humour are here in these last poems, that follow, as always, the unnerving logic of dreams. But the dream has become a nightmare, and the catastrophe, impending in all the earlier collections, has now come to pass. But help is at hand. In a late interview, Matthew cited the words of one of the writers whose work was most important to him:

> Franz Kafka in his last diary entry, on June 12, 1923, said in connection with his fast progressing illness: 'It happens whether you like it or not. [...] More than a consolation is: You too have weapons.' The weapons he alludes to were his writing and I have found the same thing.

The technique Sweeney had developed over a lifetime, and which had enabled him to compile his own peculiar *grimoire* or book of spells as protection against the full range of human terror and anxiety, now came to his aid. The poems became weapons with which to fight the arch-enemy.

And yet, the reader must ask how a poet who has been given such a diagnosis could infuse his final collection, written in the last months of his life, with such tenderness for all the world's creatures, the hunters and the hunted, without bitterness or judgement? In an inscription to one of his books, dated 11 July 1995, the poet Ted Hughes wrote these words for Matthew Sweeney: 'When among wolves, howl and devour.' Sweeney does howl in these poems, but the pain expressed is that of leaving the world behind. He lived his life with exceptional vibrancy and a huge desire for everything the world could offer him. For more than forty years, he sought to capture, in poetry, the life of a body – menaced, yes, condemned to wander, mapless, in a ruined, terrifying place – but a body fully alive to the sensuous pleasures of the world, and the vulnerability of exposure to its loss. His final poems are therefore imbued with a lyrical beauty, arising from his great sadness at leaving the world. But his spirit burned very brightly until his final breath, and the poems bear witness to that fact.

> They claim I could even still eat, with the tube
> sticking out of me, but how could I revel in
> a *Wiener Schnitzel* with that encumbrance?
>
> No, that would be like eating on the train
> to the black camp, this one with no skeletal
> survivors liberated by a victorious militia.
>
> I want to stay off that train as long as I can,
> depite all the exhortations to board now.
> I want to be myself till the last minute.

> ('The Tube')

MARY NOONAN

THE OWL

1

No one knows where I'm going,
not even me. Although that owl
I heard outside last night might
lead me to the terrain and call out
the custodians so they can
surround and welcome me, or
do whatever they want to do. I won't
speak, won't say my name even if
they try to coerce me, or play
unearthly music, such as sailors
hear far out on the Atlantic, in fog
so thick they venture to climb it
to reach clear sky. Some do and speak
of large blue birds that glide there
silently as ghosts, but those men
return too damaged to speak much
or stay above ground very long.
The owl could tell more, if he wanted
but he won't. And not only that,
he's decided he will never be seen.

2

I'm happy to honour that, but I'd like
to know what kind of owl he is.
I mean, is he blue, or is he striped
so he can blend with the forest?
Is he tall and white, from the Arctic,
or a pygmy, from further south?
Is he long-eared or spectacled? I want
to hear again the noise he made,
was it a screech, or a staccato *huhuhu*
followed by a deep drawn *whoo*,
or did it sound like wood being sawn?
I am ashamed I paid it no attention.
I did not know then he was a messenger,
albeit a taciturn one. How does he know
me, and why is he so interested? Once
a parrot took stock of me, learnt to speak
my name in exactly the tones I said it in,
mimicked it endlessly and so loudly
that I ran from my laughing friend's house
with my shrill-voiced name hurling after me.

3

Where does the owl go during the day?
How can he know I'll still be here
when he surfaces? I do take trains –
I go north sometimes, pulled by my past.
I fly to places. Will he know all this
and follow me everywhere? When can I
expect his sounds to morph into spoken
words that I understand and act on,
if I agree with him? But if I decide
to stay put, never leave the bedroom,
will he get fed up standing there
and row away through the night air,
hooting a farewell? I don't think so,
no, this fellow is here for the duration
of my stay on this enormous ball
and could tell right now how long that
will be, and what messy adventures
are still ahead of me, but his trick is
to keep as schtum on such stuff as
the wooden owl on my bedside table.

4

I've heard stories about owls, how they
appear from nowhere at the edge of things
to sit watching, usually staying silent,
but sometimes uttering a few words in
their night language we don't understand.
That's my fellow, although I don't know him.
Should I leave the house and hold my
right arm out for him to land on and turn
his big eyes on me? As if he'd be so compliant.
Or should I try to forget him, pretend
he's not there in the dark, like a tree
I hadn't noticed growing? Oh, at least
I should stop mentioning him here, but what
else can I write about? Not the journey
I'm taking that I know nothing of, not yet,
and when I do I mightn't feel like writing.
I think the solution might be to buy
a T-shirt with an owl printed on it,
a blue owl, on a yellow shirt, and write
about that small fellow to begin with.

5

What I want to learn is this – do owls
ever venture inside, to stand on a corner-
table, cock their heads to one side,
and take in completely what's going on?
There are mice here that may be welcome,
but I know my owl would be suspicious.
He'd assume I'd want him inside to see
what he looks like, to make friends with him,
so he'll be kind to me. I could promise
to wear a blindfold and say nothing,
act like I don't know he's there, but I will
know and that's enough. I think I hear
his thoughts and I'm sure he hears mine.
I feel his big eyes on me all the time.
Maybe I should start carrying the wooden
owl around with me, and practise owl noises.
When is he going to tell me what he has to?
I'm not asking for a map, but I'd like to know
where I'm headed, if not where I'll end up.
And I'd like to know it as soon as I can.

6

When I say I hear his thoughts, I hear some,
not the important ones. And here's one
of mine – if he ventured inside this house
he'd see something that might intrigue him,
a hand-knitted toilet roll cover, in rings of
purple, red, and white. Like an unknown planet
hanging in the sky. I'd let him have it, take it
back to his nest, or his hollow tree trunk, or his
half-sunken boat. I know he'll assume this
is another example of special pleading,
and I accept that. Would I do better to ignore
him, let him stay out there, like a pine cone
that remains unobserved? I saw my doctor
yesterday, he spoke of the deterioration,
and I felt the owl was hiding in a cupboard,
agreeing with every word. After that I went
to my sister's grave and the owl flew back
to wherever he's been ordered to lurk
while observing me. Maybe I should feel
privileged to have his full-time attention.

7

This morning I captured a beetle climbing
the parsley. I put him in an empty matchbox,
wondering what the owl thought of this.
Would it impact what might be unfolding?
I doubted this. I slipped on some spidery jazz
that I knew would annoy the owl. He needed
to be in control. I ground coffee beans
and made espresso. The aroma wafted through
the house. I freed the beetle to explore
the table, and when it wandered off the edge
I let it. I'm sure it survived, but I'm not bothered,
just as I know the owl doesn't care about me.
We are thrown together, all of us, by winds
that come here from far-off worlds. I sipped
my coffee, humming the tune spun through
the jazz, and I felt quite well for the first time
in weeks, even months. Was the owl watching –
had he been in contact with the beetle?
And what was their collective verdict on me?
Did it add up to more negative evidence?

8

Ok, I'm blanking him. I watched a crow today,
really admired how he operated, looking
after the young ones, his partner, none of
this spying on others. I've decided I don't like
owls, their self-absorption, or their nosiness
about people. I know which I'd rather be.
And I don't have to deal with a crow stalking me.
The owl would laugh about these thoughts.
He's been given the task of waiting to release,
when he can, exactly what I need to know
or what he can reveal. I admit he's not easy
but, shit, he's the dumb card I've been dealt
and I have to pretend I like him. Can I ask him
about the Oxford and Cambridge rowers,
or about the hairdressers the Louisianans use,
or the tiger cubs that Texans keep as pets?
The owl would make mincemeat of them all.
I wish he would hoot another noise to me.
I might even acknowledge his importance,
given my situation, but I won't reveal anything.

9

I felt the presence of the owl last night –
he was in the room with me. Not literally,
he appeared in a dream, where a blue van
struggled up an icy road, before sliding back,
in a horrible, wriggling way, to what felt
like an end. I'm not sure how it seemed so.
And I can't say where the owl was in this
little film, except he was definitely there.
This morning I came down the stairs,
expecting some sign from him. I found
a few brown feathers on a white plate
on the kitchen table. OK, then, he must be
a brown owl, but why donate some feathers,
and what did these denote? I made coffee,
then put on a CD of Anouar Brahem's oud
that seemed to suit the moment. And I
decided it was the time to poach two eggs
to serve on top of two slices of rye bread
while I primed the espresso machine again
and asked myself what the owl was saying.

10

Those feathers were gone from the plate
when I went back for them, this evening,
so I wondered if maybe I'd imagined them,
or if they'd fluttered up from the eggs
before I'd poached them. That doubt was
caused by the owl, I was sure – I'd made him
careless, and he was recovering his poise,
his control. And I was back in the place
where I knew nothing, where he liked me to be.
I opened the door and stood there, listening,
but no owl sound came. Then a bat just barely
avoided my head, and glided towards the moon.
I stood watching this leathery fellow, then
closed the door, and opened some wine.
How much did the owl control? Would I
be attacked by a rat tonight while I slept,
not savagely, but enough to terrify me?
Or would cockroaches swarm on my duvet,
clicking enough to wake me? The idea being
that these would render me so punch-drunk
I'd welcome whatever the owl had to say.

11

I spent the morning drawing owl after owl
on bits of paper, and after I'd got somewhere
near a proper depiction, I found a black marker
and reproduced this on an A2 drawing page
which I Pritt-Sticked onto the gable wall, then
I dug out my old black bow and four arrows
and unleashed these into the body of the owl.
I knew I was being provocative, maybe even
launching an act of war, but I could take no
more, and couldn't see what I had to lose.
The owl clearly was unmoved by this, so I
repeated the desecration four times over
till the drawn owl looked machine-gunned,
whereupon I flung the bow down on the grass
and went in to pour a large glass of Talisker
for the first time in months, if not years.
It still tasted good. I slipped on *Kind of Blue*,
which always chilled me, and lay on the sofa
with my shoes kicked off, and the curtains
wide open. I thought, let the owl do his worst.

12

When the dark came, I lurked in the kitchen,
bow in hand, arrows in the quiver that hung
from my left shoulder, like the Robin Hood
I wanted to play in the school pantomime –
I got Little John instead! I kept looking out at
the dark garden, wondering if I should be there,
waiting to fire arrows at any sound or movement.
Why did I want to kill the owl? He hadn't given
me the news I dreaded, but he'd stayed silent.
That was more than I could bear. I poured a
glass of Malbec and put on a CD of Baltic jazz.
Did he think I could wait forever, as if I were
a rock? I sliced some cheddar and a heel of bread,
opened the back door and went out. The moon
turned its big eye onto me, and I saw it wobble.
The stars hummed along. *Where am I going?*
I shouted at all of them. There was no response.
Then far off, I heard a faint *huhuhu* followed by
a *whoo. You cowardly bastard!*, I roared, and
sprayed the arrows all over the blackened world.

THE SEQUENCE

The Albatross

Well, I tried to walk the tightrope over
the ravine, but I fell in. Luckily, I only
broke my left big toe, and the snakes
didn't get to me before the albatross
pounced and brought me to the island
where I lay on the black sand under the sun,
tholing the pain by whistling that hornpipe
I could never dance to, even back when
I was winning medals in any Feis I entered.
The albatross perched on a rock, staring.

I could see he was wondering what he'd saved,
but he was happy to leave me where I was.
I removed my blue hat from my head and
limped over to put it on his feathered crown.
He didn't try to stop me, and after a minute
he took off and flew out over the bay,
keeping low, as if he thought the blue hat
might make the fish curious. Not then,
but maybe later. And when he returned he
sat on my foot, and the pain seeped away.

The Director

The Director sat on top of the stepladder,
pointing at the cliff. *Go there*, he said –
march, but like a beaten soldier, not a
conquering one. And make your clothes
look like a uniform. He let his loudhailer
hang from his neck, as I pinballed his last
instruction around my head. So my clothes
now had to act too? I didn't remember
this scene from the script, and where were
the rest of the cast, not to mention the film
crew? I looked quizzically at the Director,
then at the fat sun in the sky. Two gulls
on a rock laughed at me. I glanced around
to see if anyone was behind me then set off
walking, slouching towards the clifftop.
Don't seem so half-dead said the voice behind
me, *Retain some element of a march.* I did
my best to carry out his wishes, all the while
aware I was nearing the cliff. Already I could
see the big waves below. I stopped at the edge
but the shouts urged me on, so I turned,
and there he was dancing on the top of
the stepladder, looking as excited as a boy
witnessing a kitten being decapitated.

The Target

Tie me down to the target on the ground.
I watched you assemble it all afternoon,
and you did it well. First a perfect circle
of dried oxblood, then a smaller circle of
crushed, blanched almonds, then pulverised
wolfsbane – a ring of the perfect blue –
and next your secret mixture of buttercup
and turmeric. And finally, in the middle, an
orb of the most scented, brightest paprika.
I approved it all loudly, and I'm hard to please.

If I stretch out flat, I'll fit in the red centre.
Fasten my wrists and ankles to the iron pegs
with leather thongs, and please tie a green
blindfold over my eyes. I don't want to see
the two-seater glider home in on me, until
it gets so close that the woman at the back
stands up with her bow, pulls the taut string
to her shoulder, and zings an arrow into my heart.
I know she won't miss. Now what about a blast
of jazz? I'm sure you have a wine I'd enjoy.

The Assassins

I was asleep in the hammock when the dog's
barking woke me. What was bugging him?
Then I spied at the corner of the field a man
in pirate costume with a black eyepatch
walking towards me, pointing a blunderbuss.
From the opposite corner came another man
in a slick SS uniform, brandishing a silver Luger.
A cough turned my head around to witness
a woman dressed as a Wild West prostitute,
holding a cocked Derringer. The fourth corner
hosted its own little drama: a small white horse
pulling a carriage laden with a Gatling gun,
and a man in Confederate garb who quickly
turned the super-weapon around to aim at me.
I was cornered, literally. Were these my
assassins? Why the theatrics, were they all
unemployed actors? Was my dog really a dog?
I looked at the pine tree that rose at my feet –
should I leap at it and shin like a monkey?
No, I'd then get as perforated as the border
between stamps. But had any of these clowns
ever fired a gun? I lay back on the hammock,
closed my eyes and waited, but no shots came.
When the dog came to lick me we were alone.

The Ancient Crane

This morning I stood at the window
watching an ancient wooden crane,
pulled by a donkey, break down the gate
and rumble up the path, with a cage
dangling from it on a hoist rope, containing
a wolf. Driving it all was a long-eared owl
who sat tall, scowling at me, as if now,
finally, I'd get my deserved come-uppance.

I jumped back into bed to wake properly,
and when I got up again, they were gone.
That owl was a foreigner, probably Mexican
but he didn't exist, I reminded myself.
Wolves were obsolete here, and only in
Greece had cranes been pulled by donkeys,
and that was centuries ago. I needed a lot
of espresso today, and two hard-boiled eggs.

When I was leaving the house, though, I
noticed the gate was damaged, but still
hanging. And a dog-turd lay on the grass
(or was it a wolf turd) plus two speckled
brown feathers nearby on a path-stone.
There were even some flakes of rust visible.
Whistling, I hurried out onto the road,
and buttoned my coat as high as it would go.

The Exit

At first it seemed perfect: the green sea,
and a silver pony bounding towards me, as if he
was waiting to carry me anywhere in the world.
He bit me, though, took an apple chunk out of my arm,
where the blood spurted. I should have run away,
but where would I go? The road I'd escaped on
stopped dead, leaving a field where nothing grew
except marram grass. And I saw sheep eyeing me,
while baring their teeth, and crows circling in the sky.
And suddenly, out of some concealed loudspeaker,
came cackling laughter, loud enough to be heard
on the island, where they'd captured me five days
before, when I was playing chess with myself on
the tiny pier, a glass of beer warming on the wall.
I sat on the ground, covering my eyes and my ears
in turn. In the lull before the next attack (which
would come) I asked myself why I was surprised.
This was surely inevitable, and just what I deserved –
what had I tried to do to stop the teenage suicides,
for example, or girls blocked from getting abortions?
I waited for the crows and the sheep, and worse
surprises, but nothing came. The laughter stopped,
so I opened my eyes. A gate had appeared
two hundred metres away – it was black and tall,
with sculptures of owls on it, and it looked open.
I got to my feet, looking round me. I knew this could
be another trap, and where I ended up could be
worse again but I let my instinct lead me there.

Crocodile

He was in the river, as if he belonged there,
dawdling in the water with two eyes above it –
twin periscopes that flicked from one bank
to the other. I mean, this wasn't the Zambezi,
but the River Lee! I stopped to stare at him,
and that drew his famished attention to me.
Time to vamoose, I reckoned, hurrying across
the Shakey Bridge, at the end of which I turned
just in time to see him climb onto the bank
and start to wriggle up the steps. Jesse Owens'
run in the Berlin Olympics, 1936, was my model
as I crossed the road and hared past the pub
to my gate, which I firmly rammed shut, then,
after entering, slammed the door of the house.
I positioned myself at the front downstairs
window, half-camouflaged by the curtains,
sipping my glass of water, and sure enough,
two minutes later, Mr Crocodile nudged the gate
open with his snout, and let his little legs
bring him halfway up the path where he lay himself
down to wait. His tail wagged slightly like a dog's.
Was that a smile when he bared his teeth,
or was he simply showing me what daggers
they were? How on earth could I withstand him?

The Chess Match

I got a phone call to tell me the chess match
was this afternoon, in Fitzgerald's Park.
What chess match?, I asked. Come on, you're
representing your county, the voice said.
My county was at the other end of the island
and I couldn't represent a rock at chess.
And besides there was no big chess set any-
where in the park. I'd seen one in Freiburg
when I was a student – I used to sit and watch
intellectual men wage chess war over hours,
struggling to manoeuvre the giant pieces from one
square to another, while onlookers cheered.
I admit it made chess a spectator sport
but that was in Germany, *Mitteleuropa*,
not a modern Irish city, and I hadn't played
chess in decades. Even so, to my surprise,
I pulled on my black coat and dodo-skin hat
and crossed the Shakey Bridge to the park.
I'd got myself into the mood for a contest.
I thought about asking two young women if
they'd be my supporters, but they wafted by.
Maybe there'd be bus loads of loud people
wearing green and yellow Donegal scarves.
If there was, I missed them, the big chess
set too. I queued for a coffee in the hippy café
as the police car pulled up, siren blazing.
There was a bomb, we were told, we needed
to scarper. So this was yet another trap, I
realised, as I bounced along the riverbank,
like a baboon given a head start by hunters.

The Angel

I look out the window a lot, while reclining
on the bed. Oh, I turn away when it's raining
but today has been fine. I was watching the birds
flying over the university when I noticed a very
large bird among them, swooping and rising
on the thermals till it changed tack and headed
my way. In fact it came to the house next door
and perched on the chimney. Well, I say *perched*
but stood would be more accurate, for it wasn't
a bird, it was actually an angel, yet it didn't
look like any angel in a Renaissance painting.
No, this fellow came straight from 1950s Britain –
the dark tapered suit, the black suede creepers,
and the hair swept back in a quiff. He was
staring at me – with difficulty, I realised, when
he reached back and took from a haversack
a spyglass which helped him have a good look.
After he was sated he reached back again to
release a grey kestrel which he loosed in my
direction and I watched it come straight as
an arrow to bounce off the windowpane
with a sound like a thunderclap. Poor bird,
I thought, then I said *bad, incompetent angel!*
Was that supposed to be a message for me?
At that, the teddyboy took off and glided over
to smile, then veer away – even the wings
seemed suede, and were grey. I lay back
to make sense of it all, but couldn't, so I
traipsed downstairs to check if the kestrel
was dead, or had been there in the first place.

The Glider

It has snowed all morning, and the city is white
and I see a glider has landed on a neighbour's roof.
This craft, too, is white, with dark yellow moons
on both wings, and on both sides of the fuselage.
The plane sits there on the slope, nose pointing
to the clouds that have gone invisible in the swirls.
There is no pilot sitting in it, and I know for sure
I am meant to play that role, but how do I get
up there, and if I do, what will pull us into the sky?
How indeed has it managed to land so neatly there?
If I'd known about it I'd have stood at the window
all morning, waiting for it. Now I rummage in a
drawer till I find my leather gloves, then I salvage
from the wardrobe that sheep-smelling jumper
I bought in Dingle on a cold New Year's Day, and I
find on the hallstand my old leather jacket, also
my warmest woollen scarf, and on the low shelf,
a chunky knitted hat, and when I'm fully kitted out
I walk out the door to make footprints in the snow,
staring at the glider, waiting to be beamed up there.

Sweet Song

I was playing melodic jazz that had seeped
all the way from the Baltic when it cut out
to be replaced by a very loud singing that
filled every space in the house. I stood there
espresso cup in hand, thinking I'd never
been hit by anything so sweet, not even
that dawn bird symphony in Maida Vale
after a night of acid. Tears cascaded down
my hairy face. I didn't know the language
of the song but I understood it, and I couldn't
tell if the singer was a man or a woman
or an angel. The melody suggested a being
dancing alone on the moon while meteorites
swirled in slow circles around her head.
Why was I being subjected to this sublime
private recital? How long would it go on?
Should I applaud or would that be crass?
Ruminating like this at a great distance
from the music I went to lie on the carpet.
The song was long, but it kept morphing into
other songs – now it conjured the sea bed,
next the Arctic snow, till finally it stopped
so suddenly I shrieked. The Baltic gang
were at their violining and saxophoning
again but now they sounded like toneless
malevolent dwarves, mired in the world.

Crucifixion

I was boiling a beetroot when the doorbell rang.
'Who the hell is this?', I muttered, marching
to the door. When I opened it the sun was so
bright I only saw silhouettes, but that was enough
for looming over everything was a big black cross.
There were two men, one with the face of a goat,
the other a huge fellow with a fag in his mouth
and sweat on his face from carrying the cross.
The first man grinned, shaking his bag of nails
and patting the hammer in his belt. 'We've come
to carry out your crucifixion.' Seeing my reaction
he laughed, 'Don't worry it's all been paid for.'
The other man had set the cross down, and was
checking out the lawn for the best location.
'Can I ask who's paid for it?' I stuttered. 'Surely
there's been a huge mistake.' A laugh ensued.
'No mistake, sir. It was your good self exactly
who ordered the happening. See here,' he said,
shoving a signed order form into my face. It was
my name all right, but it was a forgery. I pointed
this out, to no avail, so I shouted that was enough.
'Kindly leave this premises immediately, and ask
your giant clown not to forget his cross.' I slammed
the door, then wheeled an armchair up against it,
and sat in this, after getting my biggest sharp knife.
I had my mobile primed to call the police, but I
thought I heard the two lumbering down the path,
and a look through the spyhole confirmed this.
I went back to the kitchen to check my beetroot.
It had nearly boiled dry and the water was red.

Shadow of the Owl

The loudspeaker hidden in the thornbush
is pouring out Sinatra, while a sharp light
comes on above my head, and a flurry of wings
arrives from behind me, and the shadow
of the owl covers me, then recedes into night.

I am sitting here on a log, in the *wee small
hours of the morning* (thanks Frank), reminiscing
about my student days in the Black Forest,
that ghost in the tower, and the pile of bottles
we left behind us following the farewell party.

I can still smell the marijuana, and the wine
I'm now drinking is superior, but I couldn't
fling myself around in a punk-dance like then.
I hear an *uhu*, and another, before the owl's
wings drop their poncho of shadow again.

What does the creature want from me tonight?
I thought he'd done with me, done his worst.
Sinatra is embarking on a song called 'Ill Wind'.
I empty the bottle and fling it into the dark,
enjoying the smash against the rock. I go in.

The New Lighthouse

I made my way to my new lighthouse.
It wasn't easy – the road stopped a kilometre
away, and I had to splash through a marsh.
Then the tide was in, so the outcrop
was submerged. I sat on a stone wall,
thinking this was maybe not the best start.

I was afraid the rusty key was going to snap,
but it gained me entry to dust, cobwebs
and mouse shit. And a smell like the last
inhabitant had died somewhere behind the wall.
I clumped up the circular stairs to the room
where the star of the house, the big light lived.

After a bottle of pils I summoned the courage
to unleash the light. At first the lever stuck,
then relented but not one particle of the blinding
beam soared over the sea. No, it all flooded
in on top of me and I felt like I was under
a giant x-ray that was slowly dissolving my being.

I squirmed away but there was no escape,
and bounding down the stairs I was shown not
one but three human skeletons and a dog's
behind the walls, also an axe, a long knife,
and on the floor, blood that never washed out,
spelling out *Welcome* across the stone slabs.

The Portrait Painter

She contacted me by email, I didn't respond.
She wrote to me the old way, in red ink –
I crumpled the letter and flung it in the bin.
Then she arrived at the door with her brush,
her easel, her tubes of paint, and enough
canvas to construct a tent. Time for us
to go outside, she said. She snatched a chair
from the kitchen, and forced me to sit on it
with the sun at my back. She set up her
easel and got started. Hours later I asked
for a glass of water. This had to wait
until she needed a break, and I used this
to take a peek at myself. Never in years
of looking in the mirror had I looked like that..
I started thinking of Picasso – those women
he painted, each of whom he loved. But
even though he put their eyes on one side
of their faces, the results were beautiful.
None showed beetles emerging from the mouth,
or scorpions disappearing behind the shirt,
as I'd seen was happening in my portrait.
She took up where she left off, and eventually
declared herself finished, and ecstatic – that
was the word she used. I nodded, then she
invited me to view her work, and was unmoved
when I declined. Smiling, she demanded
wine to celebrate, so I opened a Bordeaux.
I found my cheque book in a kitchen drawer
and paid her, before we bid each other adieu.

The Gallows

I was woken in the night by loud hammering.
It went on and on. Who had decided to hijack
my sleep and for what pressing reason? On my
fourth cup of tea someone rapped on the door,
making a noise like a machine gun. It was barely
light, for God's sake! I tightened my kimono
around me and went to the door to find a skinhead
in some kind of uniform waiting. He informed me
I was expected down at the river straight away,
He kindly permitted me to get properly dressed.
I had to almost run to keep up with him. Not
a single other word did he utter till we came to
the Shakey Bridge where he stopped and pointed
down to a wooden structure familiar to me
from my dreams. Do you like your gallows? he
said. It's brand new, specially built for you.
I saw a man in a red suit holding a black hood.
The noose hanging above him was white enough
to feature in a TV detergent ad. Already a small
crowd had convened, and more were trickling in.
It was like the old days of the public hangings in
the nearby Gaol. Shall we go down? my guide asked.
I sleepwalked after him and picked my way
through the gawping spectators. The hangman
shook my hand and even gave me a toothy smile
before he slipped the hood over my head,
then helped me up the steps. I felt the noose
go round my neck and tighten a little. This is
finally it, I said to myself as I waited for the click
that released the trapdoor, but this didn't come.
Five, ten minutes I waited there in silence, then
hesitantly raised a hand to remove the hood
and found myself alone. I was swaying
on the edge of an old wall above the river.

Butterflies

I haven't seen any butterflies
fluttering above the snow, but
that blackbird with his yellow beak
sitting on the hedge is not the first.
Where are the chunks of bread?
he is silently saying. Not far away
I hear the angry engines, marauding
gangs of gun sleighs, looking for me.
I'm astounded they haven't got here.
I keep waiting for a blast of gunfire –
I know their type, if they can't find
me they'll shoot someone else.
I've never been so happy I'm back
from the main road, up several
small flights of steps. Yeah, as if
that would stop them! I stand at
the window, surveying the white
garden, wondering if I should build
something out there in the snow –
maybe an enormous snow butterfly.
It would be a distraction to master the
coaxing of those big wings together.

An Invitation to Dinner

A sky blue envelope broached the letterbox,
bringing me an invitation (in cursive aquamarine
on a cream card) to a posh-sounding dinner
in a castle I'd never heard of in my part of town.
Yeah, right, I said, flinging the card on the floor
to observe that on the flip side it listed the menu.
I picked the card up again to appraise the fare.
Very interesting, I said to my stuffed hedgehog,
awaking his interest. For starters, either flash-fried
bear liver, or barbecued breast of flamingo.
The main course offered three possibilities, all
enticing. First, there was fillet of whale served
with steamed Tasmanian algae, next warthog curry
with wild forest rice, and finally, soft-shell coconut
implanted with desert vegetables and flowers.
Just the kind of menu that would make me drool.
How did they know? And what were they to me?
I looked at the address again – Castle Mada Rua.
Was it in red brick, then? How had I not noticed it –
unless it didn't exist, and this was an elaborate trap.
Some bad boys went to extreme lengths of ingenuity.
I got my thickest blue pen and wrote in big letters
on a blank page *Thank you, but I don't eat anymore.*
Then I enveloped it, and trudged to the Post Office
to put a stamp on a letter that would arrive nowhere,
before going back to fry an egg with too much cayenne.

Stench

At first it was burnt toast – well, savagely
burnt toast, the kind where the bread is all black
and snaps into angry crumbs. No amount of
shaking the toaster would yield the offender,
and nor would the smell depart. Next it was
rotten fish – no, rotten octopus (my nose
has always been a detective, unfortunately),
but where can one obtain fresh octopus in Cork?
And if you think that's bad, what about putrefying
minced pork, the kind I buy for Serbian meatballs –
had I stuck it in the fridge and forgotten about it?
There was also the ripe scent of dried ox-blood,
wafts of camel vomit, and a hint of donkey shit.
And last, *la pièce de résistance*, the unmistakable
stench of my own rotting corpse, even though
I was still above ground and able to smell it.
All these smells commingled, like a symphony.
Whoever had masterminded this, I had to take
my trilby off to him or her, and fling it out the door.
I also had to either move out or purchase a gas mask.
The clothes-peg on my nose had begun to hurt me,
the eau de cologne I'd drenched myself in was
evaporating. I felt like digging a hole in the lawn
and sticking my head in, though how that would help
was a good question. I was well beyond my last tether,
when the unexpected happened – the air took on
the pine-charged freshness of a Swedish sauna.
Coughing, I lay on the kitchen floor to digest all this.

The Drawer

I was walking down the corridor.
The sun shone in through the glass
like the smile of a long-loved friend.
It felt good to be on the top floor.

I came to the elevator, pressed
the button that made me imagine
I was blind. The whirring unseen
machinery was, as usual, magical

when it opened the door, only this
time, instead of a compartment
to stand in, I watched a drawer
slide out – it was as big as a bed,

indeed, it was kitted out like that,
with a duvet, sheets and pillows,
and blue lights on its sides flashing
as if giving me a signal to climb in.

No way, José, I said to the wall who
neither agreed nor disagreed with me.
I knew where that drawer was going
and it made sense I was in it, only I

was different – a bolshie bastard
who loathed counselling, plastic tubes,
breathing helps, or belonging to
the stricken. I was going to survive

but how was I going to get down
if no elevator came. There wasn't a
stairs. Would my belief give me wings
to fly with from an opened window

or would I have to stand here, starving,
peeing myself, for as many days as I'd
need to convince myself to climb into
the bed and let the drawer slide closed?

The Tube

Golly, a nice man wants to put a tube
into my stomach, and his colleagues
are pleading with me to simply let him.

One woman sat by my bed holding
the harmless little tube, as if the sight
of it would make me say *Yes, stick it in.*

Instead, I continued to be noncompliant.
You might as well be holding a noose,
is what I said. The woman smiled and left.

I lay there and closed my eyes, imagining
all the nourishment that would go through
the tube, reversing my super weight loss.

I would now grow fat as a sumo wrestler,
or as the beer drinker I once was, back when
my illnesses lived in hypochondria county.

I could whizz up *boeuf bourguignon* to
baby food, or even thinner, and pump it in.
I could learn to forget what food tastes like.

They claim I could even still eat, with the tube
sticking out of me, but how could I revel in
a *Wiener Schnitzel* with that encumbrance?

No, that would be like eating on the train
to the black camp, this one with no skeletal
survivors liberated by a victorious militia.

I want to stay off that train as long as I can,
despite all the exhortations to board now.
I want to be myself till the last minute.

The Sick Bed

'All this time in bed.'

KAFKA, *The Diaries*, 18 December 1922

It's a boat that wants to be a submarine.

It's a seaplane waiting for the deluge.

It's a tent wishing to be a shroud.

It can want all those things, but I'm not interested.
I feel its suction when I come through the door,
but I don't go upstairs. I make for the kitchen,
storm in, play Italian jazz loud, till Enrico
Rava's trumpet blows the blues away.
Yeah, the blues ain't just music no more, man.

And today when I've stayed indoors I treated
myself to a German breakfast – a hard-boiled egg,
small chunks of two different cheeses, rye
bread toasted, and espresso, of course, espresso!
Entschuldigung, heute hatte ich keinen Schinken...
After which I went up to lie on the bed that was no
sick bed, and it knew it. I took my laptop with me
to write on. I looked out the window at two
magpies courting on a chimney. Yeah, they were.

The bed wants me to be in it always, never leave,
so when I go to pee several times in the night
I feel it getting agitated. No, nothing like rocking,
however gentle. More a mood I sense that manifests
itself in dreams I don't like – understatement...!
Best is to abandon it completely, take an aeroplane
to France maybe, stay a whole week away.
It doesn't believe I should be doing such things.

I had a carpenter grand-uncle who once told me
his favourite creation had been a bed, *whose* bed
I no longer remember – let's say it was a dwarf
who lived in a cave on the sea shore spinning birds
out of gold thread, and these he flung into the air.
Yeah, I know that's a bit fanciful but I don't care.
The bed hates that kind of stuff, and that matters.
Like it disapproves of my writing – my weapons,
as Kafka put it. Well, I won't stop firing them, not
for a long time. I might even write about the bed.

Or should I dash out and buy a tin of yellow paint
and turn the room Van Gogh yellow, bed and all,
even the duvet? The sun might peep through to see it.
Or do I dismantle the bed, take it onto the lawn,
pour petrol on it and transform it into a bonfire?
I bet the smoke would be black. I won't do either.
The bed can stay on here like the serpent it is,
two-faced, as ever. Yeah, I've got its number,
and I will use it how I want to, on my terms.
And there's absolutely nothing it can do about that.

It's a chassis whose wheels have been stolen.

It's a dog kennel that's been knocked out of shape.

It's an escapee from a hospital ward on the moon.

Plum Saké

(for Mary Donnelly and John Mee)

The plum saké was left in a china carafe
with a design of purple flowers on it –
I found it on the low wall as I took the bin out.
One sip was enough to show how good it was
but who'd brought it here? I sat and drank,
slowly as the sunset, wanting more before
it was gone. I left the empty carafe there
and went in. I was imagining swooping in
a glider low over the ocean as I reclined
on the sofa, till the quiet ringing of a bell
brought me out into the garden to see the
carafe was full again. This time I continued
down the path to check if anyone was lurking –
any waiter or waitress in a black kimono, with
a bottle of saké, maybe brandishing a samurai
sword, with a red bowl for my severed head,
but all I met was a blind, three-legged dog.

I returned to the plum saké, and this time,
brought a chair out from the kitchen so I
could savour it better. Where could I buy
this nectar? Would I have to return to Japan?
I heard avian activity, and a long-tailed bird
with a black forehead landed on the gate.
I'd never seen one of these before. I sipped
my saké slowly as the rising moon, closing
my eyes to taste it better. Ages later I nipped in
to the little room and when I came back again
the carafe was full. I offered no complaint,
even raised my drink to toast the invisible
supplier, but I knew this was my last one,

I was not stupid. It was almost dark now,
an owl would soon join the bird on the gate.
I whistled a jagged early Tom Waits tune,
then glugged my plum saké down and went in.

OTHER POEMS

Dubrovnik

What a beautiful city! The trip was daft,
of course – all those hours travelling,
with a surprise stop in Bosnia, and no
passport (I'd left this in the hotel!), to arrive
at the high-up, ancient, walled city called
Stari Grad – somewhere I'd longed to visit.
I had no time to enjoy it, though, or take it in.
I just registered its majesty, sitting above
the Adriatic, like a tiara. What a stupid way
to visit a great city. Better not to have made
the journey, at all – (I remember I'd had to
catch a bus at 6 a.m., and waste the whole
day travelling), but hey, I went there,
spent a couple of ridiculous, aimless hours,
and no one can take this away from me.
No, I can always say I visited Dubrovnik
even if I cannot recommend any music
venues, or restaurants I enjoyed eating in.
I don't care at all if you don't believe me.

The Rain

The rain came down so hard on the dead bodies
it washed the blood away, and the murdered men
looked as if they'd wake, stand up and walk again.
They didn't, as the boy on the stalled motorbike saw,
before chug-chugging off to report his discovery.
First, though, he took five photographs on his phone.

The rain was so heavy he could hardly see the road,
or the llamas that strayed onto it. He even forgot his
favourite thing to eat was grilled llama sweetbreads.
He did know that these pictures would bring him
the reporter's job he'd left school early to procure,
and that he'd be the best journalist of the century.

The Juggler

The balls are in the air again,
twirling round the invisible sun.

I'm a juggler. I wear the green
jersey of Ireland, and orange gloves.

The blue dog sits watching me.
The plump yellow cat ignores me.

The white butterflies, as usual, try
to outdo the balls – one day soon

a planet will collide with a spaceship
and there'll be only one winner.

I have my jazz playing. It pleases
the dog and infuriates the cat.

I have eaten my allotted meal
of stir-fried tofu and black beans,

tossed with chopped coriander,
and eased down with a cup of saké.

The balls must spin for ten minutes.
They must stay at the same speed.

I imagine kings watching me, presidents,
dictators, film directors. I grin a lot.

When the time is up, I catch each ball,
secrete it in a different pocket,

then check the camera has captured
the whole revolving show, and my face

has behaved for the select crowd,
or must I do it all again? The butterflies,

by this stage, are confused, and collide
with the window panes. It is time to

feed the dog his stewed rabbit-hearts,
the cat her courgette and crispy fish skin.

Onions

I had my favourite 70s sandwich for lunch today –
you'd be good if you could guess what it was,
especially if I said I could only find it in Buncrana
on the sea, in a foodie bar called *The Drift Inn*.

No, there wasn't the tiny ghost of a prawn there,
or a slice of smoked salmon. No sardines, either
(I'm aware they swim nowhere near Donegal),
and no crab, ever, although I'd be all for that.

You'll be gobsmacked when I reveal what it was –
roast beef with tomato and slivers of raw onion,
on brown bread. Mustard was an option I always
availed of, and I think I had to have a dark pint.

Seldom the latter now. But I made the sandwich
with slices of leftover roast beef, organic tomato,
and yes, a touch of raw onion – all on rye bread.
It was so perfect I almost paused to hunt for the pint.

I compensated with two (or maybe three) glasses
of Médoc. I sat there, licking my teeth, picking
up the crumbs and sniffing the perfume on my
fingers. I knew it wouldn't wash away, and I saw

then that the onion, although sparingly used,
was the undoubted star, the Roy Keane of the team.
But that strong taste is hardly what I'd class gourmet –
some cuisines, believe it or not, excommunicate it!

Onions came up in a pub recently – a woman was saying
they were great for the blood. Yeah, I thought, recalling
Miss Doherty, my father's ascetic assistant, who ate
onion sandwiches every day and died of leukaemia.

Ballycotton

The day was hot. The cliff-walk was crowded,
my neck was playing up as usual, so after walking
a kilometre or so, I pounced on the first bench I'd
met that was free, and I sat down to watch the sea.

There were green and red kayaks, and a blue two-
seater canoe. The island sat empty, close to the shore,
and I saw a man had slid down a tall rock to stand
with a fishing-rod, not caring how he'd get back.

I became aware that I had no support behind me,
just a spreading thorn bush, whose many tiny spikes,
I knew well, carried tetanus, so I had to sit forward –
all the better to study the aerial ballet of a butterfly,

a red admiral, I felt sure, and I hummed softly in time
to her swoops, and clapped when she landed on the path
to curtsy, before rising to repeat her bonny kinetics,
this time landing on my head, as the *coup de grâce*.

Then the roving thunder arrived – a pair of pudgy bees
like doughy policemen, visiting all the dull flowers
of the thorn bush behind me, going too close to my ears,
and I knew my butterfly was far from impressed.

They drove me away, I have to admit, those bees,
and the butterfly accompanied me a bit, before
turning back to woo another walker, while I hobbled off
to seat myself in front of a plate of haddock and chips.

The Log Cabin

The log cabin has burned down again
but this time no one was in it.

People said the smoke was green,
and the flames kept in a tight circle.

I was in Chicago when I got the news.
I found a bar with a local blues band.

I asked the singer if she had a song
featuring a burned-down log cabin.

She pretended not to understand me,
then sang about warring couples, any

of whom could have torched a house.
No couple had lived in the log cabin

for at least fifty years. I knew this
because I had lived there alone

for half of that period, and the ghosts
then had it all to themselves.

The first fire was the work of the devil
though I knew I got the blame for it.

I rebuilt it with silver birch boughs –
It looked like it had fallen from the moon

I could easily believe I was up there
when I lay on the ram-skin rug,

running old rhymes through my head,
singing silly, forgotten murder-ballads.

Returning to a Borrowed House

When I came in, it was dark.
A big cat ran across my feet, or
was it a badger? Where was the moon?
The key tried not to work for me,
then relented. I fell in onto the stone floor.

I opened a bottle of red wine, and sat
at the table. I got up again to light
the six wicks on the candelabra, then
stood conducting the six dancing flames.
I launched into a homemade aria.

The lyrics I improvised were to do with
monks marooned on an island, one
of them longing for a nun on the mainland.
I introduced a psychic crow for ballast.
I felt I'd earned a slice of bread with stilton.

I sat down again and poured more wine.
The ghosts had gathered at the windows
to stare at me. I ignored them –
I was an interloper here, born and bred
in Donegal, a day's boat-ride away.

The Ice Cream Van

The ice cream van's breezy, circus music
swirled around the corner, as I left the Shakey
Bridge, with a phone charger crammed in
my pocket that I knew had a hole big enough
for coins to slip out through onto the road.

Not that I'd bend down to pick up enough
to buy a tub of this very non-Italian ice cream,
despite a sun that had risen from the canvas
to punch a few clouds, and bejewel the river.
All I wanted was a place to plug my phone in.

I was waiting for the whole world to call me –
first my doctor, with the results of my tests,
next my publisher, with news of deadlines,
and of course my partner who always rang me.
That added up to more than the world.

But as I hurried down the narrow road between
the park and the playing fields, the ice cream
van's music followed me like a fat shadow, a silly
overcoat someone was running to slip on me.
I very nearly turned back and bought a cone.

The Hedgehog

The hedgehog stood on the doorstep
looking up at me. What did he want?
Where had he scurried here from?

I wanted to put sunglasses on him
and a small yellow hat. *Hello*, I said.
The spiky fellow made no reply, but

kept looking at me as if I could read
his intent. On a whim I stood back
to usher him in. He darted past, then

dashed up the stairs. *Hey!* I shouted,
galumphing after him, to find him in
my bed, as if that was his new nest.

No, no! I muttered, reaching for him
but he turned into a ball of spikes
that pricked my hands away. I heard

clicking and hissing. Was he hungry?
The house was full of spiders, and I'd
seen traces of slugs. Should I go hunting ?

I stood watching him. It was October –
he wasn't thinking of hibernating here,
was he? His sounds now were whistling

and a kind of purring, but not like a cat.
I wished I had a cat. I wanted to know
what I had to do. Should I cook him,

wrap him in wet clay, like I was told the
Gypsies do, and bake him in the oven
for two or three hours? Or should I simply

pull on oven gloves and grab him, bundle
him down the stairs and out the door
to the hedge where I could push him in,

maybe even make him a makeshift nest
with branches torn down by the hurricane?
I asked him quietly if he would like that.

No new sounds came. He wasn't moving,
I hoped he was all right. I lay down beside him
to reflect further, and I soon began to snore.

Pizza à Sète

(for Padraig Rooney)

The wood-fired oven was as good
as any in Napoli, and the super-thin,
crispy crust was a pizza-snob's delight,
but the tomato sauce was wrong.
Where was the oregano, and why
was this replaced with *dried* basil,
making it all sweet, and persuading me
I was eating a Provençal *soupe à pistou*?
I found myself longing for torn leaves
of fresh basil and wondering why
the French even bothered to try this,
but every table was full, and most
were laden with pizza. And I knew
that Sète was half-Italian – it even used
to be called *Cette* until the Académie
Française intervened. And yesterday
I noticed the machines upgrading the port
were from Italy, while this afternoon,
in the market, I sat eating *gambas*
opposite a pasta stall called Sardinelli.
Still, I once met a man who claimed
that the word 'pizza' comes from *pissa-
ladière*, an onion tart I can buy
here in the market and that would
make all the Italian stuff derivative.
Yeah, as if I could ever forget the pizza
I had in Napoli all those jolly years ago!
Wasn't it normal to have border fights
over everything? I knew Sète was far from
the border, but it was a southern port
with a fast line to Genoa. So, devouring
my last *gamba*, and finishing the wine,

I stood up just as a large man walked
past, shouting *arrivederci* at someone
or possibly at me. I almost responded,
thinking the fellow would know all
about the art of making pizza, and
might even teach me how.

The Sleeping Woman

(after Paul Valéry)

What vile secrets are burning in you
as you pretend to be a flower ?
What weird nutrients are warming you
and presenting you as a sleeping woman?

Your breath, your dreams, your stillness
are not enough – you have to add a sniffle
because that black wave is welling so huge
before it breaks on the breast of an enemy.

Ah, sleeper, dropped here among the shadows
and the dumped, your sleep has become
a gift stretched out like a doe
beneath bunches of grapes on a vine.

So, although your soul may be off in hell,
this body of yours, with its smooth stomach
which a motionless arm is draped over,
remains watchful, and my eyes are open.

Taxi à Sète

I asked the nice man from Vietnam
to call a taxi. He'd just brought the *nem*
but this request was a high bridge on
the River Kwai I'd ordered him to bomb.
I had no idea why he reacted like that.
I was gobsmacked when he went round
all his patrons, sitting there, wielding
chopsticks, and asked each of them if they
had numbers for taxi firms. He jotted
down plenty of numbers but nobody
answered. Was it really the first time
he'd been approached about this?
All the tables had wine bottles – how
did these savage drinkers get home? I
thanked him for his failure, paid the bill,
and struggled up the hill to the flat.
On the way I remembered all the times I'd
arrived at the *Gare de Sète*, hoping to find
a taxi, but they were always in Montpellier.
Back then I didn't need one but now I did.
Anyway, I made it, and managed the
stairs, pausing on each landing, before
letting myself in to play John Coltrane.
I opened the window to share the noise
just as a taxi turned into Rue de la Révolution
to speed down past my temporary home
where it could have braked, disgorging me,
before carrying on to where it liked to roam.

Three Heads

Five hours in Carcassonne airport,
then the flight cancelled. And us put
up in a crap hotel, no food, no drink –
I saw it all as a large, grey monster,
with three waving heads. We slept,
and next morning, not without a huge
effort, learned the earliest flight for us
was three days later. So we took a
taxi to the *gare*, then a train to Sète,
which we'd just left. I closed my eyes
and watched the monster float in
through the window and hover there,
the three heads weaving their spell
that threatened to take me over, so
much that I barely registered a black-
headed man with a faint moustache
placing his red bag down before us,
asking if we'd watch it while he went
for a smoke. Right enough, the train
was stopped, but after it restarted
the bag stayed there. Then a second
head peeped into the small carriage,
casing the other bags. And the third
head came, and its mocking eyes stared
insolently at us, as if we were fair game.
Were we back in the airport melee
we thought we'd never escape from?
I decided we needed to move, and we
found ourselves standing at an exit next to
an even smaller carriage, where a man
with five cases was paying the conductor
for the tickets of the three dodgy men,
as if he was their king, and could undo

all their peccadillos. Could he undo
our Carcassonne pain? Yeah, right,
I thought. Much more likely he and his
three goons were the embodiment of it,
and we would meet them all again.

Translating Paul Valéry

When I started translating Paul Valéry
my French was so ropey I kept
dragging the poor poet into the realm of
surrealism, a place he didn't want to be,
or so I thought, until one day
I recognised he darted in there from time
to time, while pretending he didn't.
This was quite a trick, I admitted,
and I had to find ways to reveal this,
which meant my going back to Sète.
I found a flat in Rue de la Révolution,
up four flights. It was in the Arab quarter
but that was cool. On the first night I
dreamt I was a fisherman in *La Pointe Courte*
who could walk on the water, drawing
the fish after him, and as a result, I was
quite rich – which was not the case when
I woke up. Still, a view of the Meditteranean,
out of one tiny window, reminded
me I was in the South. That afternoon
I went to the Cimetière Marin
where Valéry reposed, and after a hunt,
I found his grave. I stood at the foot of it,
waiting for him to hop out and greet me,
but nothing happened. Not even a big,
fat gull landed. I trudged down, sweating,
to the harbour bar for a Ricard, even
though it was early, and I had a small
bowl of vinegary, garlicky anchovies,
which necessitated a glass of red wine.
I was tempted to have a second, but I
stayed strong. Some force was guiding me.
I traipsed past the market, witnessing

the enormous pile of dumped shells,
before returning to the flat, and digging out
the latest translation I'd been stalled on,
only to find that Valéry's ghost
had restored the touches of surrealism,
before adding flourishes that were beyond me.

The Port

A high, cold wind froze my short-haired head
as I swung my rucksack through the port,
wishing I had that grey hat I'd confiscated
when my Grandfather died – I'd had to fight for it
although nobody else there would have worn
the thing, but it didn't stop them coveting it.

Reaching one's sixties has its own rewards,
one of which is saying 'Fuck them. They'll learn.'
And if they don't, it's their funeral. No one else's.
I wanted to buy an old, white greyhound to
walk with me on a silver lead though the town.
If anyone spoke to me about it I'd stay silent.

My biggest regret is that I've never travelled
in a submarine, surfacing in this very port.
I spent my childhood days here, jumping into
boats, then back out, then learning to sing
the loud shanties the local fishermen revelled in,
though I had no idea back then what they meant.

Fernfeld

A card bearing a shot of the dark side of the moon
arrived, inviting me to a party at Fernfeld –
a big house, arts centre at the end of the earth,
at least in local terms. I'd never been there but
artist friends had landed in kayaks at the wharf
and had been treated like Picasso and Matisse.

I stood with an espresso, turning the card, as if
it would release its secrets. The poodle stared at me.
There was no address, as if that would be uncool.
I'd be expected to read a couple of shortish poems,
and no fee, or even expenses, were mentioned.
It felt like a summons from Stalin, or Putin.

I also got the feeling I should read German versions
but that could have been the doing of the house-
name. I resolved to arrive there, wherever it was,
in a red buggy drawn by a pair of white hinnies.
I'd have a faraway look in my bloodshot eyes
and my hair would be dyed the colour of the moon.

What a True Fan Has to Do

I never wanted to be a waiter in Madrid,
not even those black or red aprons could tempt me,
but when I learned a statue of Lorca had appeared
in 1998, on the poet's 100th birthday, in Plaza de Santa Ana
showing him releasing a bird to the Teatro España
I marched up with my CV to the nearest *cervecería*.

The boss was Mexican, which helped me, especially
when I told him I was an Irish poet who loved Lorca.
He was seated at an outside table, eating sausages
and I got the job when he decided I looked Aztec.
'We Mexicans and Irish go back a long way,' he said,
or I think he did. I opted for the red apron.

Every morning I went across the Plaza to greet Lorca,
wondering why he wasn't declaiming one of his poems
instead of holding a frightened dove in his hands.
Then I ferried coffees, water or even whiskies
to the seated Madrileños or intrepid tourists –
when it was hot I brought the beers earlier.

And each night I read seven Lorca poems aloud
(and once the whole of *The House of Bernarda Alba*) –
I started with English translations, then graduated
to the originals, as my street-Spanish improved.
My plan was to write the poems Lorca hadn't written
and get him world famous all over again.

The Lamppost, Plaza Mayor, Chinchón

The old matador
        and his favourite picador
stride out of the Bar la Villa,
both straight as the lamppost
in the middle of the Plaza Mayor
        that will be a bullring
later in the year.

        I sit all day here,
reading Hemingway's Spanish books,
drinking coffee after coffee
while a plaque on the wall
        informs me that in 1863
a man called Salvador Sánchez 'Frascuelo'
convalesced here from grave wounds
        caused by a young bull.

Later he became a famous matador.
I order a glass of red wine
        as the tinny bell tells me
it's eight in the evening, and the cars
begin to arrive at the Plaza to start driving
round the lamppost, going as close to it
as they dare, before chugging off home.

The kitchen opens, so I order an octopus
tentacle done on the grill, and watch
an elderly biker
        power his machine
from the ring, with full headlights dazzling
just as the lamppost comes on, its five
carriage lamps casting an orange glow on
        the red and yellow banner
draped round the Plaza, and I raise
my glass to toast the metal king.

Monsieur Lapin

(for Raymond)

Was I nine or ten when my grandpa sent me out
with his bicycle light to lamp rabbits? He handed me
a jute bag, a garrotting wire, and allowed me to
bring a friend (was it Raymond?), and Bonzo,
(a black cocker, far from a lurcher). Don't
arrive back with less than three, he announced.

Bonzo bounded down the darkening road that
brought a breeze to meet us from the sea.
We set up our stall on the dunes. I commanded
all of us to lie on our mouths and noses, even Bonzo,
who had to be held. The moon and stars were
hidden. Those rabbits would be out soon, fluffy necks

waiting for their wire necklaces. And they did come,
but Bonzo scared them off, and after I sent Raymond
down with him to the waves, so he could splash in,
two rabbits leaped around in my light like filmstars,
easily dodging my inept lunges with the wire noose
till I shrieked, and they scurried away for good.

So up the dark road we traipsed, the bicycle lamp
throwing a faint light ahead, Raymond sulking, Bonzo
whining, then in the door to Grandpa standing
in the kitchen, his knives sharpened, his oven pans
shiny and waiting. *Où est Monsieur Lapin?* he asked.
Your light wasn't bright enough, *Grandpère*, I said.

Trauma

I must declare I'm a Buddhist, yes sir, yes madam,
and this will colour everything I have to tell you.
I was having a zen evening – I'd cooked big noodles
in coconut cream, and was spooning them in, quite
leisurely, when my peace was exploded by the sudden
attack of a hoover. I am not exaggerating – it was like
a soldier had burst into the house with a flame-thrower,
razing everything in his path. I admit I was puzzled.
This was none other than my sweet partner (no Buddhist,
maybe, but certainly a fellow traveller, and no lover
of the dreaded hoover, which I would like to ban).
Anyway, she advanced noisily into the sitting room,
mopping up god knows what, taking off the brush-end
to nakedly gobble what was there. It was right then
I got curious. In the morning we were taking a taxi to
the airport to fly to Tibet (with a changeover in Nuuq) –
it was no time to clean the house. So I advanced,
gingerly, to witness what I'd class a minor war-crime.
She was sucking up small gangs of flying ants who'd
somehow gained entry to the house. I watched her,
how she'd switch the monster off and sit down to enjoy
her soap opera, with one eye on the carpet, then up she'd
bounce to hoover up the latest intrepid black marauder.
I wanted to grab the machine and put my mouth
to the tube, to suck back the little fellows, but I knew
they'd be dead, murdered, with no guilt at all, and more
mayhem would follow. I went upstairs to meditate
and the stress must have caused me to sleep, but all
night the hoover sporadically woke me and I don't know
how I'll cope with the flights, or with my sweetheart.

The Snow

The snow keeps falling
but it can't stop here.

All day the flurries have brought
their swirling white showers

that turn to slush, then rain,
as soon as they hit the ground.

The last one tried a different tack –
it pretended to be hailstones

but these, too, melted in a minute.
It must be galling for the snow

to know I'm in the house,
with no plan to leave

so it can knock me down,
then focus on covering me

till I'm ripe for the other burial,
after which the snow promises

to decorate the settled earth,
as long as I forgive it now.

As if it's that easy, I say,
whereupon the snow slips away.

The Grinners

It's when you're feeling lowest
that you meet them, the grinners,
approaching you, beaming,
like you're an old, lost friend –
you almost expect them to break
into a trot and embrace you,
but you see then it's nothing to do
with you, no it's wholly about them,
their delirious life that they must
broadcast on their faces to everyone
they meet – people who are broke
or have just been dumped, or been
given a medical diagnosis from hell.
Are they not aware that misery
makes the world turn? That their
stupid grins endanger their perfect
lives, for who wouldn't want to buy
a hatchet and hack off their heads
to lie on the pavement in pools
of blood, with the grins still intact?

The Bathroom Devils

Shit smells like corned beef
when it's kept in – those old
tins from far-off Argentina
that floated their way to Donegal
when I was a child, long before
this constipation that bedevils me.
Prunes, grapes and water should help
but don't. Laxatives are hit and miss
which is more than I can say for myself.
I should rig up a high wire from this
rooftop to the one across the street
and pay a boy to wheeze an accordion
while I inch my frame across the divide,
forcing myself to do what I can't do,
as an example to the bathroom devils
who want to stop everything and must
be taken on. Yes, a splash or two
might ensue and that would be a result.

The Heron

When I went down the hill, the heron
was agitated – screaking like it was being
killed, but flying wildly, and landing on
the grassy sides of the riverbank, then
looking back to where it had flown from,
before taking off again, and screaking more.

I stood and watched, wondering what
was bothering it, but I had shopping to do
in the Coalquay Saturday Farmers Market,
and I admit I stopped worrying about it.
When I trudged back, weighed down with
leeks, potatoes, a swede, and lesser healthy

stuff, I noticed the heron was more like its
old self, keeping still as a representation of
its outline in a Japanese woodcut, and silent
as the same, and I wondered what had irked
it so much – the seagulls? Then it took off
and flew ahead, like its world was sorted.

Tennis

The priest served the ball so hard
it bounced once, then zipped through
the wire fence and took the sea-road.
The kitchen boy was sent galloping
after it to salvage it, as usual, from
the sheugh where the road turned.

The ball was soaking, so he wiped it
on his bum, and headed back to
the tennis court beside the hotel
whose guests never played, or so
it seemed. The ball was fired over
the net and the game restarted.

Both my father and the priest wore
white gear that his housekeeper
washed once a week. I assume this,
as I was too young to know, but I do
remember my father was good, and
sometimes won, but the priest was better.

The Danube Book

(for John Hartley Williams)

I've been thinking about your long-dreamed boat again,
the one I never did see, but you sketched it for me
after dinner one night. We'd just had Serbian meat-
balls, which must have propelled it into your mind.

You began to outline your scheme, as you poured
more wine. The two of us would travel the whole
length of the Danube, filling notebooks with poems,
recipes, anything else that caught our fancy. We'd

moor the boat each evening and sample the local
fare. Oh, yes, we'd have a companion on the trip –
that Croatian friend of yours from the island of Braĉ,
who'd been handling boats like yours his whole life,

and who'd know what delicacies to ask for when
we dined, and whichever wine might suit best.
You may have said he had a repertoire of songs too,
from all along the route, and these were for the book.

It was you alone, though, who'd take photographs,
only black and white. We'd try to find poems to translate
whenever we stopped – using some kind of grapevine
you remained vague about. The book had to be fat

when it was launched in a fireworks display on the bank
of the Danube in Novi Sad, where you'd spent some years
in your 20s, and where you would now return in lights,
clutching a shiny copy of your long-dreamed Danube book.

The Descent into Limbo

(i.m. Pieter Nijmeijer)

Pieter, someone – was it yourself? – has sent
me a postcard I wrote to you in March 1992.
On the picture side we see Mantegna's
depiction of Christ climbing down into Limbo.
He looks a bit like you. Is that where you are now
(though I know Limbo has been abolished)?
You wouldn't care about that. Why send my old
postcard back to me? What stamps did you use?
In my handwriting I say I can't be sure I'm
deciphering yours enough to get your address right
but I must have. You've included no address this time.
I know I gave you carte blanche to contact me in a
variety of ways, including carrier pigeon or crow,
but this method you've chosen is the oddest,
even if it seems the simplest. And if you respond
to my words here you'll recall I ruled out telepathy,
not that you'd try that. No, your way will be careful,
sure, as you always liked to be. Do you remember
being in a car with me, passing slowly through
Newry during an Orange parade? I was laughing at
how silly they looked, with their hats and sashes,
and I went to open the window to tell them this.
You stopped the car and asked me to get out,
whereupon I desisted in my clowning and we
continued in silence on our journey to Donegal.
That was before 1992. Last time we met was, I think,
in 2003, in Antwerp. I took a train from Rotterdam
to find you sitting outside a bar. I saw your damage,
immediately. Was this a pretaste of Limbo? If that's
where you are, I need to know – you choose how.

No-Man's-Land

(after the artwork of Caspar Walter Rauh)

The dead are putting on a play tonight
(or is it a film?) in no-man's-land. We'd
better attend – though what awaits us?

A bright light appears in the sky, allowing
two corpses to lurch into view, then fall
into the mud, one on top of the other

before rising again to repeat their act.
Is this all, I mutter to myself, at their fourth
go, until they get up and stagger away.

Then a huge creature in big boots dances
past two black crosses, grinning, and booms
out, deafening us, *Ich bin der Kriegsgott.*

At that, a giant screen is fixed to two broken
trees, and is lit from behind, while the other
light is extinguished and we hear gunfire.

This is replaced by the shrieks of a horse
and we see he's been spiked by a branch
while a pair of petrified frogs looks on.

A big man crosses the screen carrying a small
man whose hands and feet have been blown off.
A new explosion is heard not far away.

And here is the profile of a man's head hanging
from a tree that a snake's wrapped around.
Now we're shown Death himself, bent over, crying.

Two men are seen looking into a cave, that
seems to be the inside of a body, shining a lantern
without succeeding in finding the giant heart,

and a second pair of men are searching for God
in a church, one craning his neck through a window,
the other straining to lift a corner of the roof.

For the finale, Death appears again, this time
wrapping a ragged cloak around an erect skeleton
as a black bird flies off with something in its gullet.

The screen grows blank. The big light comes on.
We applaud gingerly, and those of us who still can
wend our grateful way out of this no-man's-land.

The Mountebank

The bear handled the pogo stick like a pro,
if there are such pros, and I loved
his luminous, purple waistcoat (his only
garment, discounting his copious fur).
Who was the curly-headed boy whistling
the tune that made the bear jiggle
round the lampposts and leap over plants?
And who was the girl with the money bag?

And why was no film camera pointing
at him, and why were no pens scribbling?
Monsieur Baudelaire would have loved him,
Picasso too – remember the *saltimbanques*?
And when the boy did a cartwheel onto
the bear's back the whole crowd roared,
the buses stopped, the taxis beeped, and
the girl conjured up three more money bags.

LAST POEMS

Tree Trunks

(after Kafka)

For we are like tree trunks in the snow.
Push them, and they'll start rolling,
it seems, but that doesn't happen
because they're wedded to the ground.
This, too, of course, is an illusion.
Still, they stay piled up where they are.

Coloured Hair in the Garage

(for John Morehead)

A big man wearing a hat and a bandage
over his right eye beat me to a table in
the Coffee Doc. I found another while a
male doctor walked past with green hair,
then a female doctor with orange hair.
I sipped my espresso, watching doctors
of all ages and sexual orientations hurry
on to their appointments, all with hairs
touched by the rainbow. I saw four blues,
two yellows, three scarlets, three pinks,
and one purple before I stopped counting.
All the doctors in this human garage
were at it. And I could see straight away
what it meant – their hairs were smiles
shoved up to the tops of their heads
which would help them deliver any news.
And if they smiled at the same time, well!
I had to admit it was a canny ploy, one
somebody in the HSE had dreamed up,
and had probably been well paid for.
And we would, of course, cover the cost.
Nodding, I got to my feet to call a taxi.
On the way I saw a sign saying *Karate*
for Beginners. Let me out here, I said.

The Builder's Singing

(for Kieran Crowley)

The builder is throwing out snatches of song
between his sawing and drilling. I can hear
the sun outside in his voice, also the faint
wingbeats of starlings. The words that reach
me are unfamiliar – has he written them?
Am I to assume he wishes to take his place
on a stage, and this very private recital
is a kind of audition? Well, I'm all for him
bowing out there to rows of wild applause.
More sawing now, and no it doesn't go with
the singing, nor does the drilling that follows.
I could tell him all artists have to deal with this,
the compromise of genius. Should I set up
a secret recording device, then edit out
the machine noise? Radio would see a story
there, one of the people aspiring to more.
I'm certainly going to take a slug of whisky
and tiptoe into the arena of transformation
to stand at his feet with a pen and notebook,
so I can be the first fan to get his autograph.

Hook Head

I thought I'd die on Hook Head,
I felt so ropey, and I'd slept precious
little the previous night, but I survived –
I even admired the dumpy, Norman lighthouse,
the oldest in Europe maybe, and I observed
that among the cars parked along the beach
were French camper vans. And I noted with
amusement the sign offering Hook Hypnotherapy –
yes, this was the place for that kind of carry on,
and I was very nearly tempted, but the road
led onward, and the sun beat its slow drum-
roll on the tar, the Dunbrody Abbey maze
failed to capture me, none of the bright,
busy pub gardens lassoed me, all the tractors
of Wexford couldn't slow me enough
to keep me close to Hook Head.

Homage

(for Mary)

A snow leopard cub slinks into the garden
to sit there, silently, looking at the door.
Then he stretches out on the stone path,
his gaze fixed and patient. A black tom-cat
peers through the gate but stays where he is,
and two magpies have a dekko from a wire
but our arctic fellow could be carved out
of quartz, so complete is his indifference.

Yet he's focussed on one imminent event
and you oblige on cue, by opening the door
to stand there in a regal white dress, with an
angled white cambric hat, and white suede
kitten heels set off by crystal ankle bracelets.
The cub is on his feet now and purring, as he
comes to pose beside you, and any garden
gnome would conjure a phone to capture this.

Phlegm

(for Greg Bradley)

My acupuncturist said *Phlegm is a fucker*
before sticking in needles to help flush him out
and indeed, I found it easier to catch him
over the next few days – my best was a grey
manifestation I should have photographed
and put on a Wanted poster, a wispy, spectral
desperado that was trying to drag me down
as I coughed and retched over a double tissue,
heart racing like a runaway train – the normal
picture that resumed in all its deadening glory
as the acupuncture session faded away.
So attempts to sleep were abandoned while
I descended the stairs to rack my airwaves
without waking anyone, or the film was paused
as I fled to the kitchen and closed the door.
The captures were getting rarer all the time,
and none were clear enough for photographs.
I'd have to go back to my acupuncturist and say
I agree, *Phlegm is a fucker*, can you help me
nail him and clear him out of my chest for good?

Mouse Sandwich

(for David O'Meara)

After they gave me morphine
following the incident when my heart
stopped for eight minutes and a bunch
of doctors in red suits attached
a loose curtain of coloured wires
to my body, I woke up in intensive care
to later try to sleep again, a very
light, broken sleep, full of weird
dreams. In the first of these
I was eating a sandwich on a riverbank,
and when I was nearly finished I saw
it featured a hairy slice of mouse.
And yes, I gobbled this, and it was good.
The chef was señor Morphine.
I won't tell you about the other dreams.